Planetary Intelligence:
101 Easy Steps to Energy, Well-Being, and Natural Insight

By Simeon Hein, Ph. D.

Illustrations by Ira Liss
and Peter Sorensen

 Mount Baldy Press, Inc.

Planetary Intelligence: 101 Easy Steps to Energy, Well-Being, and Natural Insight

Mount Baldy Press, Inc.
1942 Broadway, Suite 314, Boulder, CO 80302
303.440.7393   www.MountBaldy.com

Second Edition: September 2006
Printed in Canada by Friesens
on Rolland Enviro Edition recycled paper

Publisher's Cataloging-in-Publication

Hein, Simeon.
  Planetary intelligence : 101 easy steps to energy,
well-being, and natural insight / by Simeon Hein ;
illustrations by Ira Liss and Peter Sorensen. -- 1st ed.
    p. cm.
  includes bibliographical references.
  LCCN 2004102803
  ISBN 0-9715863-5-7
  ISBN 0-9715863-4-9

  1. Self-actualization (Psychology) -- Problems,
exercises, etc. 2. Nature, Healing power of.
3. Cosmology.   I. Liss, Ira II. Sorensen, Peter (Peter
R.) III. Title

BF637.S4H44 2006   158.1
                    QBI05-600104

Table of Contents

Acknowledgments

Thanks to Mantak Chia, Ray Dodd, Kathi and Hobie Dunn, Emily Faulkner, Victoria Fullerton, John and Jane Hein, Dan Hoffacker, Shino Kataoka, Ron Kenner, Ira Liss, Denise Lynch, Minori Murata, Penny Roberts, Lisa Rosen, don Miguel Ruiz, Ron Russell, Peter Sorensen, Teri Southworth, John Starman, Sharon Steinhauser, Graham Van Dixhorn, Joleen Van Peursem, Randy Weiner, and Mark Winstein for inspiration and help with this book. And to Jasper and Lucky, for their endless exuburance and boundless energy.

vi

Introduction

"The farther that one goes out
from one's self, the less one knows."
- Lao Tsu, *Tao Te Ching*.

This is a book about learning to
listen to the quiet voices inside and
around us, voices that we often ignore.
By learning to listen, we can rediscover
the wisdom and magic of nature, and
the intelligence of the planet. When we
were children we could hear these voices. But as we grew older, we stopped listening and replaced our subtle, internal
intelligence with the endless chatter of
social judgements and cultural conditioning. Our minds became the home of
a mental program written by someone
else. As a result, we became isolated and
alienated from ourselves and nature's
intelligence.

Ever since we were very little, we
have been put into a box made of ideas,

attitudes, belief systems that make us
feel small, limit our personal identity,
and distort our sense of well-being.
Fitting into these systems, bureaucra-
cies, and other mechanistic processes,
entrains us to unnatural rhythms and
patterns. Our attention is taken away
from ourselves and is instead placed on
social constructions and belief systems
that do not serve us. We become fearful
of life outside of this box and this fear
drains our energy.

The purpose of this book is to
show you how to use simple, natural
activities to remedy these distortions
in your sense of well-being. Many of
these activities involve slowing down
and paying attention to life around or
inside you. As the interactions in our
daily lives speed up, the quality of the
information in those interactions goes
down. We feel a hunger for a complete-
ness that only arises from integration
and coherency: two qualities that are

not supported by high speed of modern life. Speeding things up creates a lack of connection to ourselves and the larger universe.

No matter how many years we spent in school, we may still be undereducated in terms of our "planetary intelligence." Our schooling and education have led us to be aware of our economic and "useful" qualities, but not those aspects of awareness that simply exist unconditionally. We have been conditioned to look outside of ourselves for happiness. Thus, we have become entrained to the rhythms of organizations, machines, and beliefs rather than our natural environment and its resonance.

Very subtle bioenergetic-signals are responsible for coordinating our connections to other living things. In order to feel this connection with the natural world around us, we need to slow down and increase our self-awareness of our internal energy processes.

What is Planetary Intelligence?

The past few hundred years have seen an unprecedented evolution of technology. While technology has labor-saving benefits, it also creates an accompanying loss of awareness of our connection to the rhythms of nature. Though our great, great grandparents could farm, navigate, or hunt without relying on complex technologies, we have become dependent on sophisticated, external technologies to do these things for us. As a result, we have lost our sense of inner connection with the planet and the temporal cycles that are the basis for millions of years of human evolution. We now live in an "age of missing information" (Mckibben 1993). We have lost the awareness and information that contributes to the feeling of being part of a larger, living system.

Planetary intelligence is a physical and energetic awareness of our body and its connection to the world and uni-

verse around us. It is an innate under-
standing of our relationship to all other
living things and our sense of place on
the Earth. Rather than focussing our
energy on all the social agendas and
ideas of what we think we are supposed
to be, it is our ability to be sensitive to
the moment and all the different forms
of energy that life contains. Nature contains lots of information which comes to
us through our bodies, not our intellect.
Using our planetary intelligence, we
become aware of the multitude of rela-
tionships that support life on our planet.

Our world of technology and material
objects are increasingly driven by
efficiency criteria. Despite all the
material abundance around us, we often
feel an inner hunger and desire for
contact with something that is hard
to define. This inner craving can often
take the form of addictions, to food or
entertainment, or an undefinable thirst
for satisfaction or contentment. And

the more we try to fill this thirst, the emptier we feel.

Increasingly we live in a virtual reality, the collective product of many individual electronic systems communicating and interacting through massive, networked systems. While this machinery may satisfy an economic need for easily available short-term information, it does so at the expense of our physical and physiological well-being. While we used to be more physically active, we now spend many hours a day sitting in front of a television or computer screen. No amount of electronic interaction can substitute for being outdoors in the sunshine and experiencing the changing patterns of nature. The random, interpersonal violence that is present in our lives attests to this imbalance. We must find a way to better balance our virtual with our physiological and planetary needs.

Tapping into the Matrix of Intelligence

The matrix of intelligence is a collective, global phenomena that is the product of the network of animals, plants, and other types of awareness. We have been taught as a society to see intelligence as the product of our own individual minds. In this way, intelligence is defined as something reducible to the capacity of a brain in a single person. Some have suggested that intelligence is related to our emotions and thus have coined the term "emotional intelligence" (Goleman 1997). However, the idea here is that intelligence is the product of an entire system and is not something that we can possess "individually." Rather, it is a relationship between oneself and all the information and energy in that system.

We are all intrinsically interconnected with all the other organisms on the planet, whether we realize it or not. We

13

can only survive for a few minutes without oxygen that is produced by trees and plants, a couple days without water, and a couple of weeks without food. Every breath we take reconnects us to the matrix of planetary intelligence. And it isn't only the material resources we need, it is the energetic properties of these materials too.

Without the awareness of our connection to the other living systems on the planet, we feel increasingly alienated, disconnected, out of place. We feel an inner emptiness that we try to fill with more stuff. We substitute speed and quantity for quality. Thus, being aware of planetary intelligence has many benefits one of which is to increase the amount of information available to us: not just to our brains, but also to our bodies.

Recent medical research shows that our brains and bodies are inseparably linked together to form a "body/mind."

Every thought we have creates chemicals in our bodies. Conversely, those chemicals communicate information to all of our cells. The cells communicate with each other in the form of a huge, biological internet. The idea of a separation between our bodies and our minds is a myth of the old mechanistic paradigm.

Every thing, organism, or animal is a blend of physical and informational patterns. Planetary intelligence is our awareness of the subtle information that every being adds to the whole system, beyond its obvious "usefulness." Our lives transcend economic functionality and, to be whole, we must pay attention to all of ourselves.

In order to connect with all the beings in the system, we need to adopt a flexible rhythm that is universal to the other organisms and the planet as a whole. The rhythms of the machines and electronic devices that we are

15

normally attuned to won't do this for us
because they are designed for efficiency,
not for maximum interconnectivity
with other components outside their
limited boundaries. They are just too
controlled. In fact, these devices entrain
us to artificial rhythms that are alien
to the temporal patterns that we have
grown accustomed to for the last few
hundred-thousand years. To feel a deep,
inner-connectedness, we need to slow
down to a speed that is common to the
whole planetary system.

When we work with the energy of
the planet, it allows us to open up our
ourselves to a wider range of frequencies that in turn boost our "planetary
potential." Once we increase our personal energy, we enhance our connection to planetary information.

We tend to think of the Earth solely
as a physical or biochemical entity. But
another way to perceive the Earth is as
an enormous, energetic generator that

has its own rhythms and cycles. By feeling connected with the Earth, humans can access information as we have been doing for millions of years. Through the process of synchronized oscillations—that is, feeling entrained to these vibratory patterns—we can share information with everything else that is vibrating at the same frequency. This isn't hard to do. We just need to act and live within the present with unconditional awareness.

The universe is filled with a background intelligence that our current way of living and technology obscures by decomposing its complexity. This book is about how to be receptive to that information, and entrain with it, through simple, pleasurable activities. We are all "bio-crystalline resonators," and by using our awareness we can tap into the resonant intelligence of the earth itself. This intelligence works through our bodies and intuitive mind,

17

not through our rational, calculating mind.

Planetary intelligence is automatic. Unlike logical intelligence, we don't need to put tremendous effort into developing planetary intelligence—we merely need to focus our attention on the resonant, playful type of activities described below. When we get out of our own way, the feelings and sensations from these activities effortlessly create their own intelligence in our bodies. By restoring the connection to our own natural energy fields, our interaction with the Earth's energy fields are automatically enhanced. The simple activities outlined in this book automatically help you to regain that awareness.

Perceiving Shapes in Time and Space

Nature often creates shapes with irregular, circular, or spiral patterns. It is people and organizations that are always trying to straighten everything out. But perhaps there is an intelligence in apparently "disorganized" patterns that we don't logically understand. Suppose nature designed these shapes with intrinsic functionality that goes deeper than the surface? How can we connect with that type of energy?

Our bodies and many other things in the universe are built around spirals. Much has been written about the ubiquity of the phi-ratio, or "golden-section," as it is sometimes called, in sacred geometry and living systems. It seems that intelligence in the universe designed us around spiral patterns—such as the shape of the inner ear or our heart muscles—to pass as much energy through these systems as possible or to attune them to specific frequencies and vibrations. When objects are spiral-shaped they naturally pick up energy and information. Spirals, then, are a form of natural technology—if we pay

19

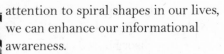

attention to spiral shapes in our lives,
we can enhance our informational
awareness.

We don't necessarily have to physically build spirals around us, but, simply
be aware of where they occur in space
and time. Spirals in time occur through
our repetitive motions and activities.
Imagine what your daily life would
look like if you filmed it with time-lapse
photography. Our physical movement
would appear as circles and spirals. This
is the secret to martial arts and medita-
tion practices. We can all benefit from
spirals by being aware of them.

Just as we see shapes in space, the
rhythms of our lives create shapes in
time. The shapes in time are the patterns of our lives. What do these patterns look like? Why do they matter?
Our patterns are mostly determined
by external routines, not our inner
need to connect with the universe. We
have been trained to live by using time

extensively, trying to do as much as possible. By consciously changing these patterns, we can connect with the intelligence around us. The intelligence "out there" can only get " in here" when we create "resonant synchronization." To resonate with nature's intelligence, we can practice activities that capture the chaotic dynamics of nature.

We are always trying to extend ourselves outward. In this book, I encourage you to consider an alternative, intensive use of time: that is, finding time within yourself and exploring it from the point of view of your physical body and the body of nature.

Entrainment with Nature— Cultivating Planetary Intelligence

Entrainment simply means that the vibration or oscillations of two different objects become similar when they come in contact or interact. We are constantly and automatically entraining with

21

all the other people, objects, and events around us. The more we are surrounded with machines, the more we entrain to their oscillations. Likewise if we spend more time in nature, we entrain to those rhythms. Because of the prevalence of machines in our world, we have unintentionally created routines that are not necessarily compatible with our innate biological rhythms. Therefore, we should create opportunities for our bodies to entrain to more natural rhythms. By doing so, we entrain to our own inner being and our natural self. This aspect of ourselves is spontaneously connected to nature and our planetary intelligence.

Being an Extension of the Planet

Our calculating minds are geared toward fast, economic rhythms and industrial functionality. However, our bodies operate on a slower time-frame that is geared to the rhythms of nature such as day and night, waking and sleep. Minutes and seconds are a recent invention as far as our bodies are concerned. With the increasing prevalence of microelectronic technology, based on nanoseconds of electronic time, it is more important than ever to pay attention to the older, larger, less-frantic cycles of planetary life. These large-scale patterns are everywhere, however we tend to ignore them because they are so slow. By focussing on large-scale rhythms we feel a sense of perspective that make our personal issues feel less important and worrisome. We perceive ourselves as an extension of the planet and in so doing, also experience the long-term patterns that stretch and expand our awareness.

Power vs. Coherency

As human beings, we have a fascination with gadgets and technology. We tend to think of these devices and machines as being outside of ourselves. Yet the

most advanced technology is already
built into us even though we may not
be aware of it. This "inner technology," which may be even faster than a
computer, does not always operate in a
linear or predictable way. And in order
for it to work properly, we need to take
care of our physical bodies for natures'
information to couple and mesh with
our bioenergetic machinery.

Modern machines are designed to
operate in predictable ways and need
a constant supply of energy. However,
what makes the inner technology of our
bodies work is not only a steady flow
of energy, but also coherency, self-or-
ganization, and spontaneous integration. This organizing process is natural
and automatic, but we can also help
to create the conditions that foster its
development. Coherency arises when
all the parts, no matter how small, are
connected and in alignment with each
other. When all the cells in our bodies

operate this way, we call it a state of "good health." So instead of only focussing on sheer, physical power, as we often do with machine technology, we can also learn from subtle, "low-energy" information. This arises from our inner coherency and creates higher-order awareness within us.

Getting to Know Your Body Again— Taking Care of Your Animal

All of us have been brought up to experience the world from an exclusively logical and rational viewpoint. This makes us overly programmed and cerebral. When we think about things in such a linear way we cut ourselves off from our bodies. We stop paying attention to our physical selves and, as a result, we become separated from our subconscious minds. We then feel anxious and uncomfortable because we are not listening to our bodies.

To contact planetary intelligence, we

need to be completely in our bodies. By experiencing pleasure, and feeling that we deserve pleasure without having to "earn it," we can become aware of our body's inner dialogue again. By sensing the world through our body, we will get in touch with the subtle signals of the planet that we are usually too busy to hear. Subtle, planetary information comes through our physiology, not our intellect.

Many people have had the experience of taking care of pets. Sometimes, however, we take better care of our pets than ourselves. We have different standards for judging the value of various types of animals, and for some reason we often judge the human animal differently from other animals. The end result is that we devalue our subtle-senses.

Paying attention to our bodies can allow us to have a direct connection with the source energy of the universe.

We receive such information directly rather than through the distorted belief systems of our socially-habituated minds. Our intuitive powers work from our subconscious awareness and its connection to our larger environment. This type of intelligence is more fleeting and subtle than logical thought: take time to work with it at its own pace.

Finding Your Hidden Power— Do Less, Accomplish More

Our present-day technology is based on the idea of taking existing resources and boiling them down to simpler products. Just like a dam in a river, something that was originally wild and energetic is transformed into a placid, controlled pattern. In our domesticated lives we have become used to overly simplified energy-patterns. Planetary intelligence, on the other hand, is created directly from nature's life-force rather than through excessively-filtered energy patterns. We can interact with this intelligence without simplifying the signal or throwing away information. This involves intentionally cultivating varying, diverse forms of life rather than destroying them. For example, in a forest the trees, birds, and animals are visible to our eye. But they wouldn't be there without the intelligence of the bacteria in the soil which are too minute and numerous to count both in quantity and type. We perceive the larger creatures only because all the smaller creatures "lower down" on the food chain are doing their job.

So instead of degrading or destroying the signal lines, like conventional, mechanistic technology, planetary intelligence enhances the fidelity and complexity of existing signals. It adds information to the whole system without distorting it. This preserves the informational diversity of the source and does not generate entropy or disorder like conventional, energy-consuming technologies.

Crop circles, those complicated, artistic patterns that appear in grain crops around the world, filter the background energy of the Earth through a crystalline lattice-work of wheat stalks. These stalks then begin to oscillate in an organized way, and they create a large-scale coherent resonance pattern which attracts and communicates with other types of energy forms with the same resonance. So instead of degrading or destroying an information signal, crop circles channel existing energy into new patterns. And as a result, many unexpected events, like electronic malfunctions and battery failure, happen in and around crop circles.

Breaking free of the conditioning that causes us to have a limited self-view, we will rediscover our inner power. In other words, we can reconceive of ourselves as planetary beings, not

just social beings. When we transcend
our ordinary identities, we gain a larger
perspective of ourselves as inhabitants
of space-ship Earth on which we are
literally flying around the universe all
of the time.

Experiencing the Unique You

Following the simple activities in this
book, you will regain an awareness
that you had as a child. Cultivating this
awareness, you will enjoy that unique
sense of spontaneity, joy, and immediacy
you once took for granted. You will feel
more alive, integrated, and in touch
with yourself. Our natural self automatically knows what behavioral response
is the most appropriate and life-sustain-
ing in any situation. We don't need to
think too much about these actions as
our natural self works instinctively and
subconsciously.

This awareness will lead you to a
greater, deeper connection with your-

self and the world around you. You will feel like the "real," expanded you again.

Fine Tuning Your Resonance with Non-Specific Intelligence

Every action and thought we have makes a difference in our lives. All of the actions and thoughts we have add up to create our life experience. The key to fine-tuning our resonance is to have more of our daily life lead in the direction of personal expansion, rather than contraction. To experience this expansion, ensure that all of your actions are coherently placed into the larger framework of your entire life. Every action counts, no matter how small. The resonance and vibration of those actions must be finely-tuned so that they are energetically consistent with everything else in our life. Look for activities that make you feel expanded, excited, and bigger.

31

Oceans of Magic

The universe is a cascading ocean of sounds, vibrations, and experiences. Rather than experiencing the daily humdrum of existence, we can turn that ocean of energy into a magical place full of synchronicities and healthy, challenging experiences. All matter is just sound waves and light in a solidified form. The waves crash across our consciousness as daily events in our lives, and larger events on the world-scale. By constantly seeking to expand our awareness, we can harness the energy of those waves to create a unique, mysterious experience every moment and wake-up every day full of expectation and awe.

Throughout our lives, we experience miracles that our minds rationalize away with ordinary, logical explanations. Given a choice between limited and unlimited belief systems, we will often choose the limited beliefs because they are safer and more comfortable.

The next time you experience something magical in your life, take the time to consider what it means to you, rather than letting the conventional beliefs of our ordinary consensus-reality automatically explain things away.

Being Sensitive to Natural Information

Our personal point of reference is usually based on our social and economic status or recent news events. By stopping for a moment, you can be aware that you are on a planet that is part of a solar system, that is part of a galaxy, that is part of a universe. Therefore we are always moving, always spinning. By some estimates, we are moving in 11 different directions at once. The only reason we do not feel a sense of wonder every second is that our belief systems are standing still. Therefore, our whole universe looks as if it is standing still. Our senses create a deceptive illusion

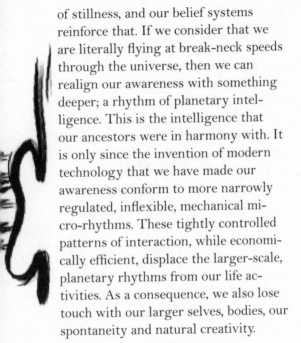

of stillness, and our belief systems reinforce that. If we consider that we are literally flying at break-neck speeds through the universe, then we can realign our awareness with something deeper; a rhythm of planetary intelligence. This is the intelligence that our ancestors were in harmony with. It is only since the invention of modern technology that we have made our awareness conform to more narrowly regulated, inflexible, mechanical micro-rhythms. These tightly controlled patterns of interaction, while economically efficient, displace the larger-scale, planetary rhythms from our life activities. As a consequence, we also lose touch with our larger selves, bodies, our spontaneity and natural creativity.

Another Type of Vibration

We are very familiar with the vibration of economic production. But there are other essential vibrations that we also need to be connected with. We are "con-nection creatures," that is, we were born to connect to everything through our sensory organs and our body/minds. Our education and social training have conditioned us to accept a much more limited existence.

Our bodies are always receiving infor-mation from the Earth and the larger universe. However, noisy social and technological signals often overwhelm our planetary intelligence. By getting rid of the energy distortions in our physiological system, we can receive the natural signals more clearly. By entraining ourselves with the temporal rhythms of the planet, our bodies will naturally process planetary information and we will regain our inherent etheric abilities.

Giving Something Back

An important part of feeling connected to planetary intelligence is to complete the cycle of energy transformation by giving something back. All of us have been conditioned to think mostly about what we can get out of life. But if we also think in terms of what can we can contribute, we will naturally entrain with the Earth's intelligence and spontaneously get the information we need. Giving and taking are two sides of the same coin. By focussing on what we can give, we will expand into the planetary awareness around and inside of us.

The Other Side of the Human

Ultimately, the purpose of this book is to encourage you to pay attention to your hidden connection with the Earth and the living things around you. It is enough to simply put your attention on the following activities for them to activate your subtle-senses and ability to listen to the quiet signals of the planet. And by listening more carefully to the intelligence of the planet, you will find

yourself more closely attuned to your true potential. You will rediscover your natural self.

Instructions

Pay attention to one of the following activities everyday, and then watch the changes that happen in your awareness in daily life. Spending just a few minutes a day on any of these activities will change your metabolism and eventually your whole life. The longest journey starts with a few steps. When those steps are taken with complete awareness, the journey will always be meaningful and fulfilling. You are on your way to regaining your unique, expanded self. Be present and go there with your full attention.

Activities for
Your Body-Mind

Go for a nature walk;
settle your mind

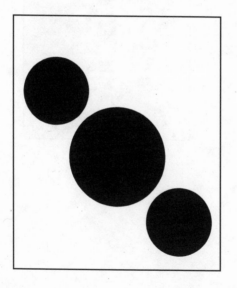

**Visit an aquarium or zoo;
animals can help you feel
connected to earth energies**

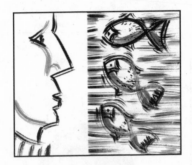

Practice tai chi or chi kung

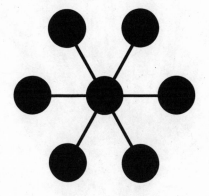

Visit a sacred site

Play with your pets

**Get to know fruits and vegetables,
carve a pumpkin**

Eat natural food

Cook your own food over an open flame

Drink lots of water

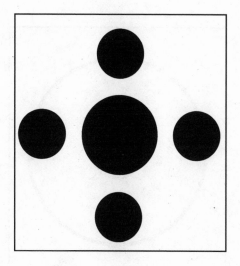

Practice sweeping, grinding, rocking motions

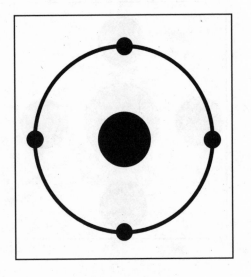

Walk in a labyrinth

Eat healthy

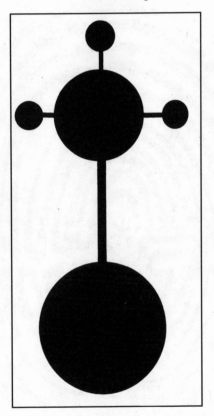

Walk slowly, slow down

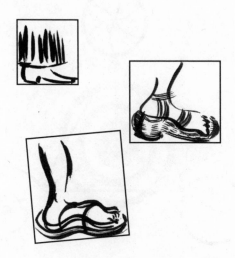

Celebrate your body

Get a massage

Take a mineral bath;
visit a hot spring

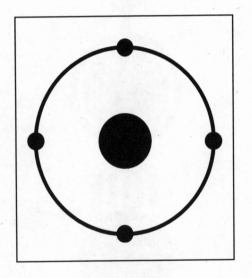

Practice daily exercise

Laughter

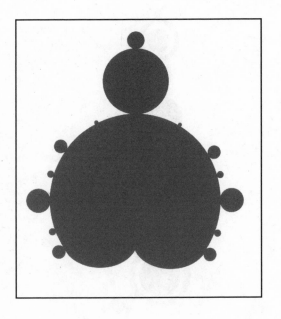

Get enough daily minerals and other nutrients

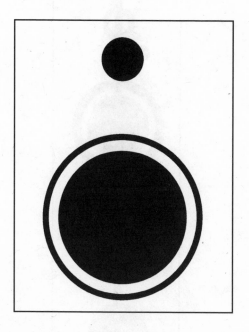

Take care of your body

Practice tantric activities

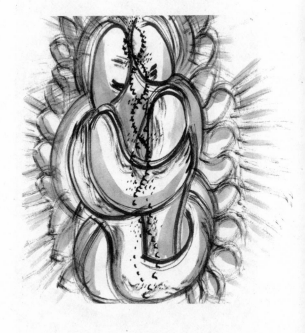

Dance

Set aside time for sleep

Create action

Climb in a gym

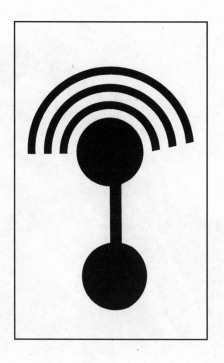

Climb a mountain

**Feel a connection to your food;
grow your own or eat local foods**

Eat consciously

Activities for
Your Spirit

**Sharpen your intuition;
take a class in remote viewing or
other type of intuition skill**

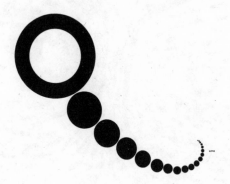

Meditate with a tree

Create your own dream

Be creative

Be spontaneous

Pray and play

Meditate

Develop your intuition

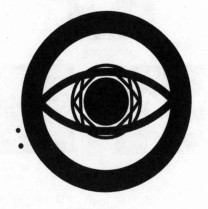

Dance in the rain, play in the mud

Practice the inner smile

Play an imaginary game
with a child

Activities for
Your Senses

Close your eyes, open your mind

Look at the stars

Swim naked in natural water

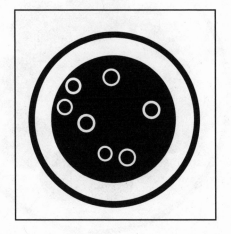

Write a song

Listen, be quiet

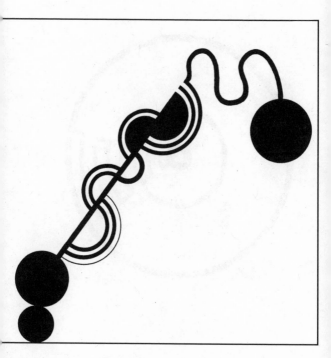

Sing

Look at the sky

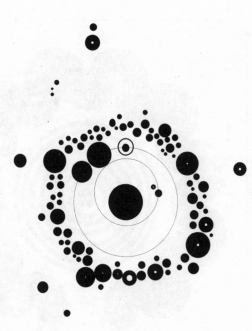

Cultivate a garden

Walk along a river

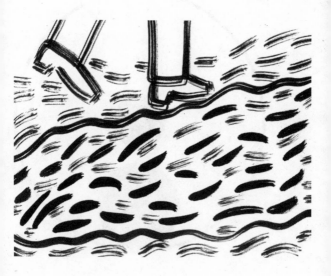

Experience silence

Sleep in the dark

Use candles

Build a sand castle
or make a snowman

Make a fire

Bake bread, kneading the dough yourself

Listen

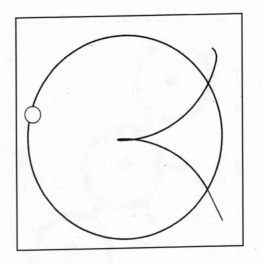

Sketch, draw, and paint

Reconnect with your
internal compass

Walk barefoot

Things to Pay Attention To

Have fun, lighten up

Breath

Spend time for yourself

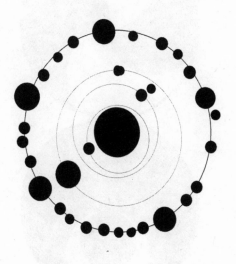

Be nice to yourself

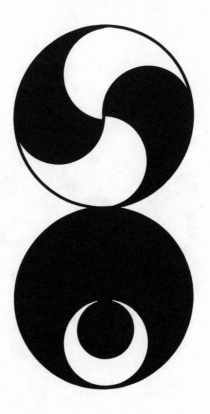

Listen to things that are good for your ears

See things that are
good for your eyes

Feel your feelings

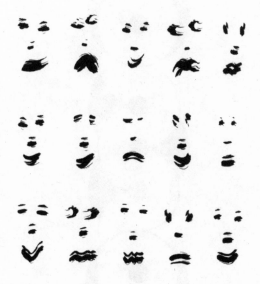

Play games

Be curious

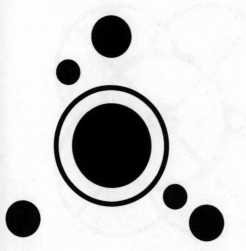

Watch the weather

Accept yourself completely

Be aware of mechanical thinking

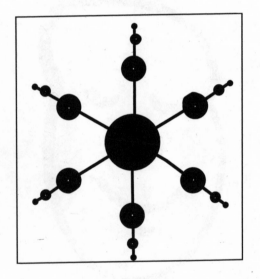

Be aware of your emotions

Consider the life around you

Take some time to do nothing

Practice Feng Shui

Appreciate What You Have

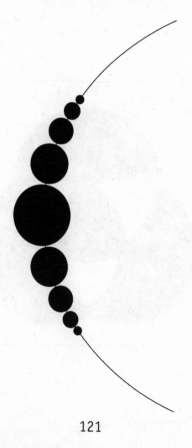

Get simple

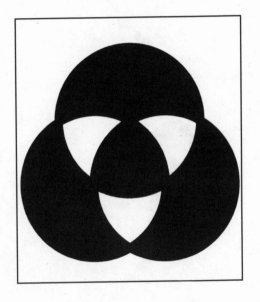

Be in the present moment

Focus on the feeling

Excite your imagination

Use visualization to see yourself moving through space

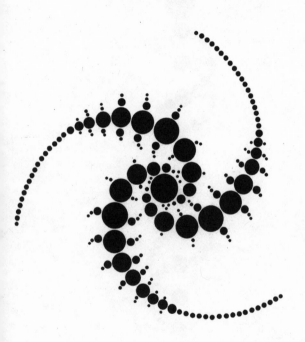

Design magical shapes

Imagine Spirals

Pick up a Rock

Recycle

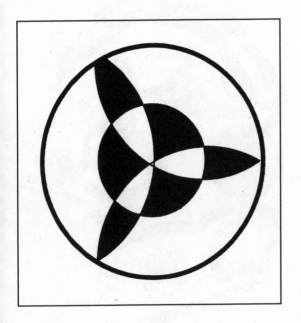

Experiment with sacred geometry

See the whole world as your home

Follow your excitement

Pay attention to your dreams;
explore them in the present

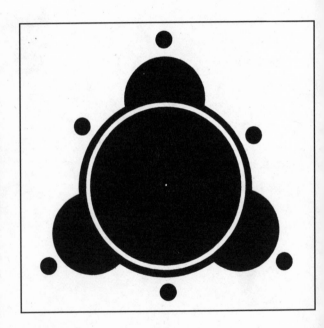

Leave a gift for the earth

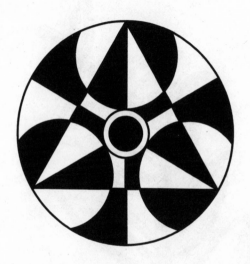

Nurture a growing plant

Make your gifts
instead of buying them

Things to Avoid

Be aware of linear thinking

Be aware of judgment

Don't be influenced
by negative people

Give yourself a day
without a watch

Turn off your TV/computer

References

Carlson, Richard and Joseph Bailey. 1997. *Slowing Down to the Speed of Life: How to Create a More Peaceful, Simpler Life from the Inside Out.* New York, NY: HarperCollins Publishers.

Chia, Mantak and Dirk Oellibrant. 2004. *Taoist Astral Projection: Chi Kung Healing Practices Using Star and Planet Energies.* Rochester, Vermont: Destiny Books.

Chopra, Deepak. 1995. *The Way of the Wizard: Twenty Spiritual Lessons for Creating the Life You Want.* New York, NY: Harmony.

Damasio, Antonio. 1994. *Descartes' Error: Emotion, Reason, and the Human Brain.* New York, NY: Avon Books.

Goleman, Daniel. 1997. *Emotional*

Intelligence: Why It Can Matter More Than IQ. New York, NY: Bantam.

Hein, Simeon. 2002. *Opening Minds: A Journey of Extraordinary Encounters, Crop Circles, and Resonance.* Boulder, CO: Mount Baldy Press, Inc.

Honore, Carl. 2004. *In Praise of Slowness: How a Worldwide Movement is Challenging the Cult of Speed.* San Francisco: Harper Collins.

Langer, Ellen J. 1997. *The Power of Mindful Learning.* New York, NY: Addison-Wesley Publishing.

Leviton, Richard. 2001. *The Healthy Living Space.: 70 Practical Ways to Detoxify Your Home.* Charlottesville, VA: Hampton Roads Publishing Company.

McKibben, Bill. 1993. *The Age of Missing Information.* New York, NY: Plume.

Pearce, Joseph Chilton. 2003. *The Biology of Transcendance: A Blueprint of the Human Spirit.* Rochester, Vermont: Park Street Press.

Roberts, Jane. 1995. *The Magical Approach: Seth Speaks About the Art of Creative Living.* Novato, California: New World Library.

Ruiz, Miguel. 2004. *The Voice of Knowledge: A Practical Guide to Inner Piece.* San Rafael, CA: Amber-Allen Publishing.

Strogatz, Steven. 2003. *Sync: How Order Emerges from Chaos in the Universe, Nature, and Daily Life.* New York, NY: Hyperion.

Targ, Russell. 2004. *Limitless Minds; A Guide to Remote Viewing and Transformation of Consciouness.* Novato, California: New World Library.

About the Author

The author at age 4 in Central Park, New York City

Dr. Simeon Hein is the director of the Institute for Resonance, a non-profit in Boulder, Colorado which specializes in resonant viewing instruction and crop circle research (CropCircleScience.com). He is the author of *Opening Minds: A Journey of Extraordinary Encounters, Crop Circles, and Resonance* (OpeningMinds.info) and composer of the CDs *Earth Dreaming, Opening Skies,* and *Dancing Man.* To learn more, visit us at ResonantViewing.org.

Quick Order Form

Planetary Intelligence: 101 Easy Steps to Energy,
Well-Being, and Natural Insight.
by Simeon Hein, Ph.D.

By mail: Send this form to
Mount Baldy Press, Inc.
P. O. Box 469, Boulder,
CO 80306-0469
Email: Orders@MountBaldy.com

By phone: 303.440.7393

www.PlanetaryIntelligence.com
Also available as an eBook

Enclose cash, check, or credit card information for $9.95 per book
(plus $0.74 tax for Colorado residents), and $3.00 (add $1.00 for each
additional book) for Priority Mail shipping. International, add $10.00 per
book (estimate) for air shipping (add $3.00 for each additional book).

Yes! I want ____ *Planetary Intelligence* books.
Please send them to the following address:

Name:_____

Address:_____

_____

_____

Phone:_____

Email:_____

Credit Card_____

Exp. Date_____

Signature_____

Quick Order Form

Opening Minds: A Jounrey of Extraordinary Encounters,
Crop Circles, And Resonance.
by Simeon Hein, Ph.D.

By mail: Send this form to
Mount Baldy Press, Inc.
P. O. Box 469, Boulder,
CO 80306-0469
Email: Orders@MountBaldy.com

By phone: 303.440.7393

www.OpeningMinds.info
Also available as an eBook

Enclose cash, check, or credit card information for $19.95 per book (plus $1.49 tax for Colorado residents), and $3.00 (add $1.00 for each additional book) for Priority Mail shipping. International, add $10.00 per book (estimate) for air shipping (add $3.00 for each additional book).

Yes! I want ____ *Opening Minds* books.
Please send them to the following address:

Name:_____
Address:_____
_____
_____
Phone:_____
Email:_____

Credit Card_____
Exp. Date_____
Signature_____